SUPER SHARKS

LEMON SHARK

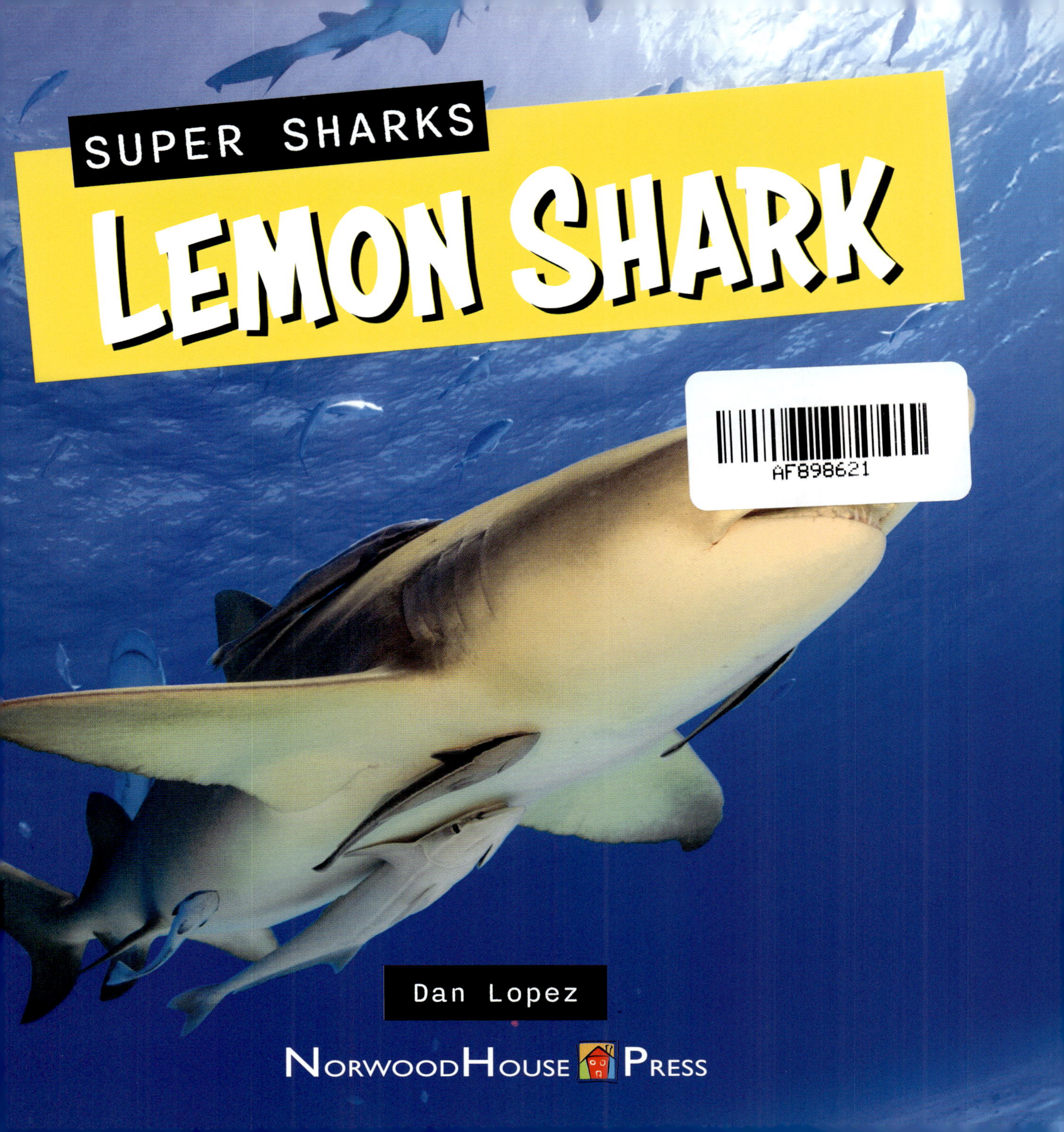

Dan Lopez

NorwoodHouse Press

Cataloging-in-Publication Data

Names: Lopez, Dan.
Title: Lemon shark / Dan Lopez.
Description: Buffalo, NY : Norwood House Press, 2027. | Series: Super sharks | Includes glossary and index.
Identifiers: ISBN 9781978581371 (pbk.) | ISBN 9781978581388 (library bound) | ISBN 9781978581395 (ebook)
Subjects: LCSH: Negaprion brevirostris--Juvenile literature.
Classification: LCC QL638.95.C3L67 2027 | DDC 597.34--dc23

Published in 2027 by
Norwood House Press
2544 Clinton Street
Buffalo, NY 14224

Designer: Rhea Magaro
Editor: Tricia Hoffman

Photo credits: Cover, pp. 1, 4 nicolasvoisin44/Shutterstock.com; p. 5 Mike Workman/Shutterstock.com; p. 6 David Keep/Shutterstock.com; p. 8 Kris Wiktor/Shutterstock.com; p. 9 aaroncraftphotography/Shutterstock.com; p. 10 Michael Bogner/Shutterstock.com; pp. 12, 21 Rob Atherton/Shutterstock.com; p. 14 Yann hubert/Shutterstock.com; p. 15 A Cotton Photo/Shutterstock.com; pp. 17, 18 VisionDive/Shutterstock.com; p. 19 Maui Topical Images/Shutterstock.com;

Printed in the United States of America

CPSIA compliance information: Batch #CSNHP27: For further information contact Norwood House Press at 1-800-237-9932.

TABLE OF CONTENTS

What Is Special about Lemon Sharks? 4
What Do Lemon Sharks Look Like? 6
Where Do Lemon Sharks Live? 11
How Do Lemon Sharks Hunt? 16
How Do Lemon Sharks Reproduce? 20
Glossary 22
Thinking Questions 23
Index 24
About the Author 24

WHAT IS SPECIAL ABOUT LEMON SHARKS?

Lemon sharks are named for their yellowish-brown color. It provides **camouflage** for living in sandy areas near the coast.

These sharks have a long history with humans. People fish for them. Divers swim with them. They are often kept in large aquariums.

WHAT DO LEMON SHARKS LOOK LIKE?

Lemon sharks are big fish! Adults grow to about 10 feet (three meters) long. They weigh about 200 pounds (91 kilograms).

Lemon sharks have flat heads. Their **snouts** are short and wide.

In most sharks, the front **dorsal fin** is much larger than the one in back. Lemon sharks have two dorsal fins that are about the same size.

Where Do Lemon Sharks Live?

Lemon sharks live in the Atlantic and Pacific Oceans. They like shallow, **tropical** waters. They swim near **coral reefs**, in bays, and at the mouths of rivers. They can survive in fresh water.

Lemon sharks swim among **mangroves** in Florida. They are found along the coasts of Caribbean islands. In many places, it is against the law to catch lemon sharks.

Unlike many sharks, lemon sharks are **social**. They live in groups. They learn from each other.

Most sharks need to swim in order to breathe. Lemon sharks can rest on the seafloor. They pump water over their **gills**.

How Do Lemon Sharks Hunt?

Lemon sharks hunt at night. They do not see well in the dark. Luckily, they have **sensors** on their bodies that pick up electrical signals from other animals.

Lemon sharks hunt for fish, stingrays, and **crustaceans**. Sometimes, they catch seabirds.

These sharks snap up prey with their teeth. They thrash their heads as they tear off chunks of meat to swallow whole.

How Do Lemon Sharks Reproduce?

Before giving birth, a female returns to the place where she was born. The water is shallow and protected. She gives birth to live babies, or pups. Up to 17 are born at one time.

Glossary

camouflage (KAM-uh-flahzh): a disguise or natural coloring that lets animals hide by making them look like their surroundings

coral reefs (KOR-uhl reefs): large underwater structures that are made from the skeletons of tiny sea creatures and that provide habitat for many ocean animals

crustaceans (kruh-STAY-shuhns): sea creatures with hard outer skeletons, such as crabs, lobsters, and shrimp

dorsal fin (DOR-sl fin): a flat, thin body part that sticks up from the back of a shark or other marine animal

gills (gilz): breathing organs near a fish's mouth that extract oxygen from water

mangroves (MAN-groves): tropical trees that can grow in salt water and that have tall, tangled roots; mangrove forests are important habitats in which many animals raise their young

sensors (SEN-surz): body parts that detect and measure changes in the environment and send information to an animal's brain

snouts (snouts): the front parts of animals' heads that include the nose and mouth

social (SOH-shuhl): preferring to be with others instead of alone

tropical (TRAH-pi-kuhl): related to parts of Earth that are always hot and rainy

Thinking Questions

1. How did lemon sharks get their name?
2. Where could you see a lemon shark?
3. How are lemon sharks different from other sharks?
4. How does a lemon shark's body help it hunt?
5. Where are lemon sharks born?

Index

colors 4
fins 9
food 18
fresh water 11
groups 14
name 4
people 5
pups 20
size 6
teeth 18

About the Author

Dan Lopez lives far from the ocean in Indianapolis, Indiana, with his wife and three kids. He is fascinated by all of Earth's animals, including sharks! He admires their sleekness and speed and thinks more people should appreciate them.